Embracing Calmness

The M.L.E. Program Using Midline Exercises

Dr. Jennifer Dustow

Copyright © 2018 Dr. Jennifer Dustow

All rights reserved.

No part of this publication may be reproduced, distributed, or transmitted in any form or by any means, including photocopying, recording, or other electronic or mechanical methods, without the prior written permission of the author, except in the case of brief quotations embodied in critical reviews and certain other noncommercial uses permitted by copyright law.

Editing by Kimberly Lee
Graphic Design by Chanel Dustow

Printed in the United States of America

First Printing, December 2018

ISBN-13: 978-09835697-0-1
ISBN: 0983569703

DEDICATION

I believe we must prepare our children, even when we want to protect them from the world they live in, because one day we will not be here and they must take steps forward on their own. Therefore, this book is dedicated to those that seek a gentler way to redirect behaviors, while in a storm.

CONTENTS

	Acknowledgments	i
1	WHERE DID IT ALL BEGIN?	1
2	NOW WHAT?	10
3	THE H.A.P.P.Y. EXERCISES	15
	References/ Resources	28
	About the Author	30

BEFORE WE BEGIN

For me, beginning this conversation on the MLE program, some of my basic fundamental beliefs must be shared first. In this case, I'd like to share my thoughts on how we are all part of a system. This concept, to me, starts with our own personal bodies (which are truly miracles), then expands to being on a planet that belongs to a breathtaking Solar System. This is important to share, because at the root of my choices and biases is the belief that, 'I am always part of something greater than myself.'

To scale this thought process back a bit, consider this, if we are unable to interface with our own mind/ bodies, comprehending our place in a larger system can really never occur. In other words, if we are not in a healthy relationship with our own mind/bodies, being part of a larger discussion is really impossible.

Let us take for example, a child within a classroom who cannot focus on the subject matter due to his or her behaviors (or as I like to refer to as a lack of brain interfacing). The outcome is that this child is in conflict within his or her own system which gets played out in the classroom environment. It is not that he or she does not want to, but rather cannot participate within that outer system, leaving the teacher unable to teach the child. All the while, the child's peers are generally left confused as well to how to connect with him or her. This child's basic system is not working for him or her, but rather against him or her.

Many years ago, a child I worked with explained it to me as being on a run-away pony. No matter what she did or tried, she couldn't get her pony to listen. This was a powerful insight shared with me, which led me on a journey into the world of brain/ behavior/ thinking/ problem-solving.

With the consent of the child's parents, we began to explore non-drug options to help her. What I found was, by providing this child with some basic, simple, and fun bilateral or midline exercises (she could self-administer to redirect her own off-task behavior/ thinking), she became the driver, the master of her basic system, her thinking. A calm mind is open to ideas. I knew that this idea needed to be researched on a larger scale. It is interesting to note that at the time, I was entering the dissertation aspect of my doctorate. Was this fate?

Before we go any further, it is important to explain what bilateral and midline exercises are so we continue to be on the same page together.

Bilateral and midline, essentially mean the same thing, just using different letters – kind of like cat versus feline. The exercises cross the midline of the body. An Occupational therapist (OT) uses these types of exercises for stroke victims to get their left and right hemisphere (fancy word for left and right sides) of the brain to communicate (Davis, 2016). What I found through my research (which in now translated in 27 languages) is that off-task behavior for children diagnosed under the Autism Spectrum occurs when their left and right brain hemispheres are not communicating. But, through introducing bilateral/ midline exercises, their brains can make the necessary connections, resulting in on-task behavior (Dustow, 2007). I will be getting into all of that in chapter one.

However, let us rewind a bit, back to being part of a system. The reason being, I want to share with you the outer systems I belong to. One of those systems is the team that made this project possible. The women in this team are slightly crazy and funny, but model infinite kindness, always mindful of the power of being a parent, and just how messy that looks most days. They are amazing, and I am humbled daily with their presence in my life.

Then, there is my husband of over 30 years, the strength in his belief – "She will be right," far exceeded my five year projection of our union. My intensity of 'being,' can be way too much most days for most people.

"Life is really simple, but we insist on making it complicated."

- Confucius (551 – 479 BC)

CHAPTER 1: WHERE DID IT ALL BEGIN?

This all began for me over 14 years ago, when I was completing my doctorate in education. My dissertation topic was, 'Do bilateral exercises that cross the midline decrease off task behavior with special needs preschoolers with a diagnosis under the autism spectrum within a classroom environment on the island of Oahu, Hawaii.' (Dustow, 2007)

Yes, I agree that is a huge way of saying, does crossing the midline of our bodies influence our behavior? But, in the academic world, exact and wordy is a must. Nonetheless, my study in 2007 was conducted in 20 classrooms with a total of 88 preschoolers.

To ensure that I did not influence the outcomes, great measures were taken under the direction of my doctoral committee, who were amazing. So, this six-week study was conducted on random days decided by a daily coin toss. However, every school day during the six weeks, off-tasks were measured through a tallying system. Those behaviors were aggression, both verbal and nonverbal, eloping (running off or away), flopping (dropping to the floor) and inappropriate talking, non-focus (zoning out) and noncompliance (not listening).

From my readings, working in the field through my private practice and cutting edge research, I believed that crossing the midline with simple exercises, the brain could be stimulated to make different choices. For children diagnosed under the autism spectrum, their greatest gift becomes their greatest concern – their ability to focus.

If their attention is to get a need/ want fulfilled, the behavior that they are expressing may not lend to being redirected in a manner that serves them. For example, if a child wants to play on an iPad but it is not an appropriate time. The child's focus is on the iPad, and will remain fixated on this need/ want at all costs. We all know what is it is like when someone wants to talk to us when we are angry. No message can be received. In fact, we will act out against that person trying to talk to us.

In order to create a system to receive messages, a calm brain must be present.

So, how do we prepare these children to receive a message in a situation where reasoning is not present? Bilateral/ midline exercises. In my research study, I posed six hypotheses regarding midline exercises. All of those hypotheses were proven. Meaning, that off-task behaviors can be decreased when midline exercises are used to redirect the thinking/ brain.

Now, this is where I provide all kinds of charts and graphs of those findings. Do not worry, I will explain what each one means.

So, here we go.
Breathe, and turn the page, you've totally got this.

The numbers going from 0 to 160 on the side of the chart are the number of possible acts of aggression. The letter on the bottom represents the coded classrooms (to endure confidentiality for the schools and students).

Now, for what this all means, the color red refers to the number of acts that occur when midline exercises were not preformed that school day. Whereas, the blue is the number of counts for aggression when the midline exercises did occur with the students.

As you can see for the school, coded AB, the difference was profound.

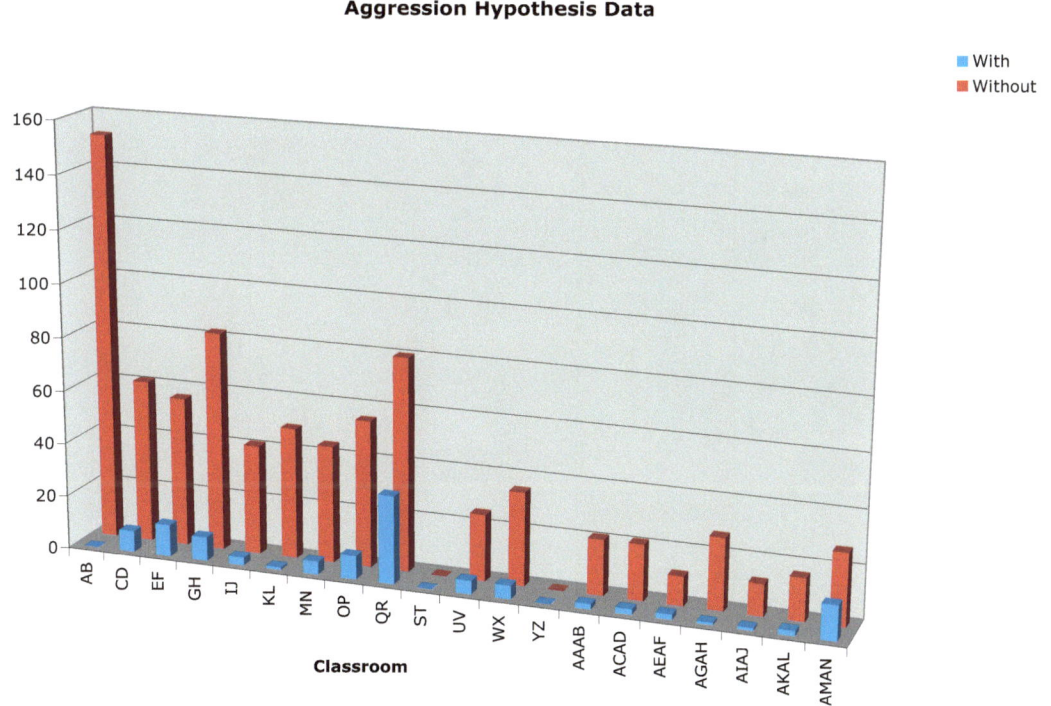

It is important to point out that the data was only take during a small window block of time and does reflect the entire school day. Now, on to the next charts.

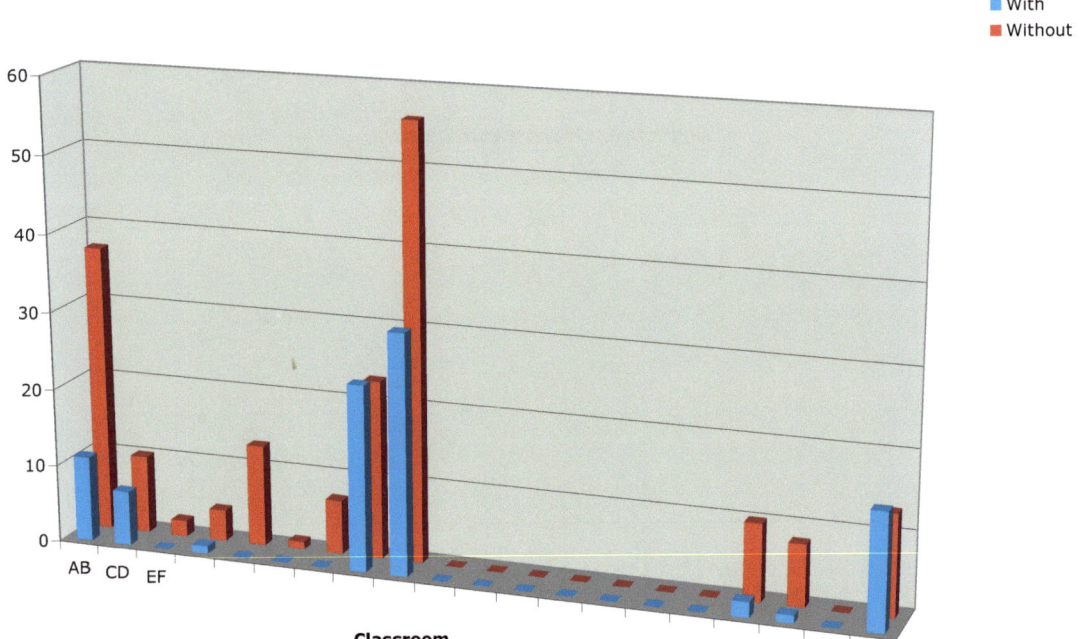

The same is true for this chart, too. Numbers 0 to 60 represent the number of possible acts, whereas, the letters represent coded schools. Remember, eloping is a fancy word for running off or away. Eloping was not a shared concern for all the schools, but for the schools that this was a concern for, the intervention of midline exercise had an impact. Except for one school, the numbers remained the same.

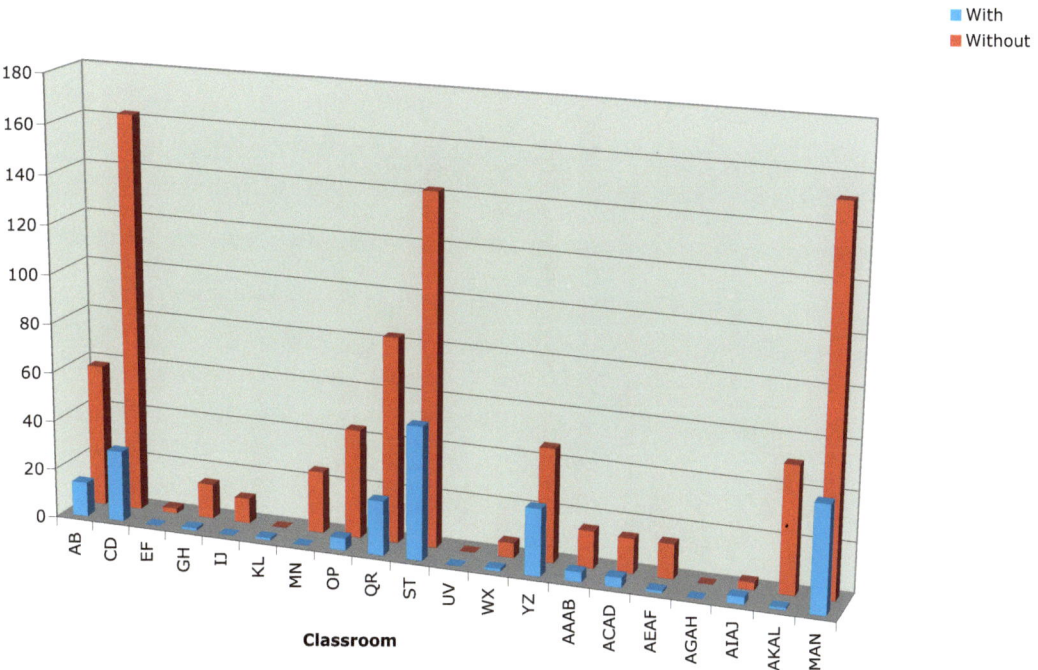

Now that you are becoming an expert at reading these charts, the 0 to 180 are the acts and the letters represent coded schools. The flopping is a term used to group the behaviors of dropping to the floor when it is not desired or appropriate. When the midline exercises were conducted, the flopping behavior decreased dramatically for some schools.

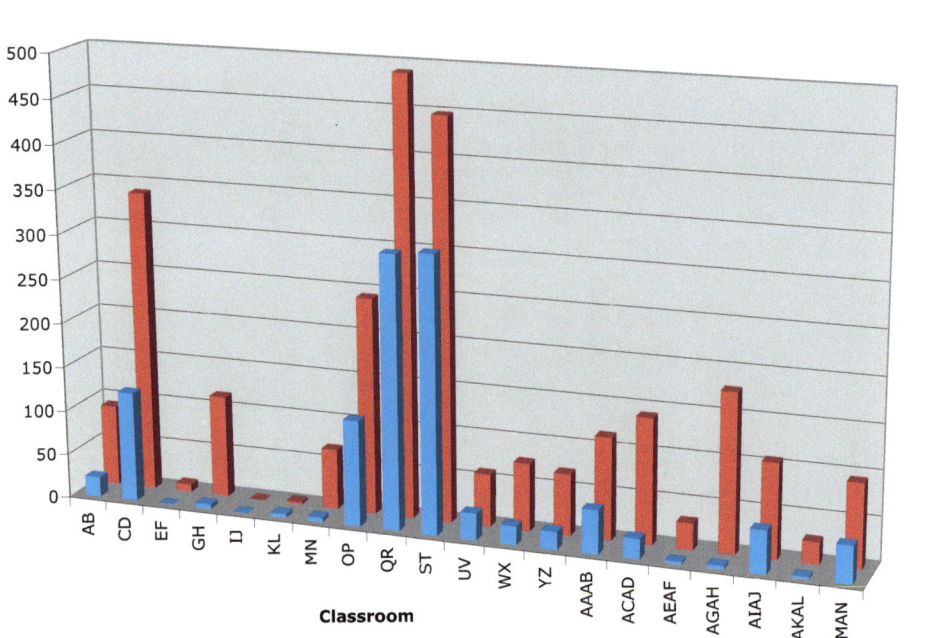

What does the numbers 0 to 500 indicate? Exactly, the number of acts. I do not even need to ask what the letters represent, you've so got this. However, what does TK represent? Great question, it refers to talking. By talking, it means when the student shouldn't be speaking or talking in class, for instance, mimicking their favorite cartoon character instead of listening. Remember, the **red** indicates when the midline line exercises were not performed that day.

So, now you're so ready for the last two charts, non-focus (staring off in space) and non-compliant (not listening and doing their own thing).

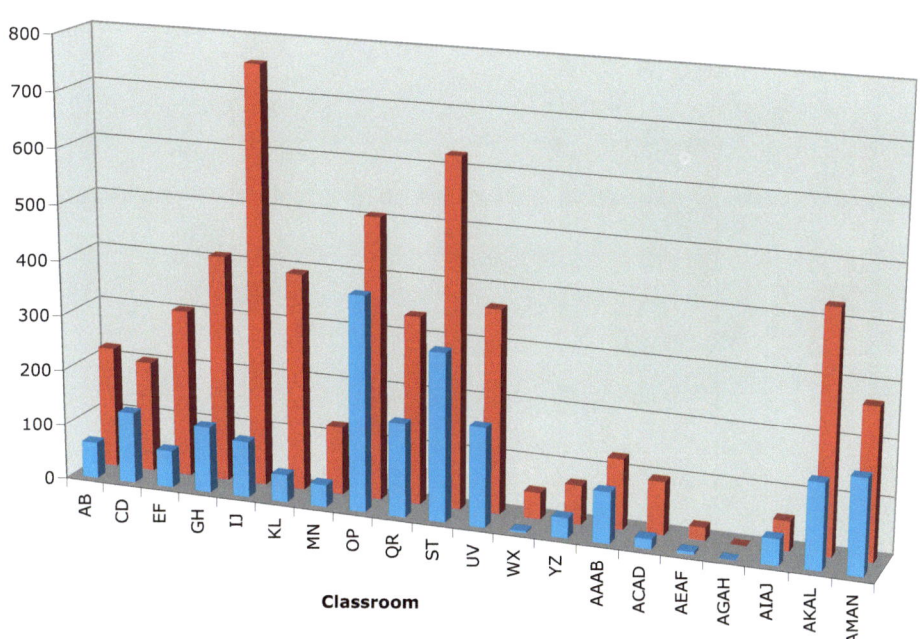

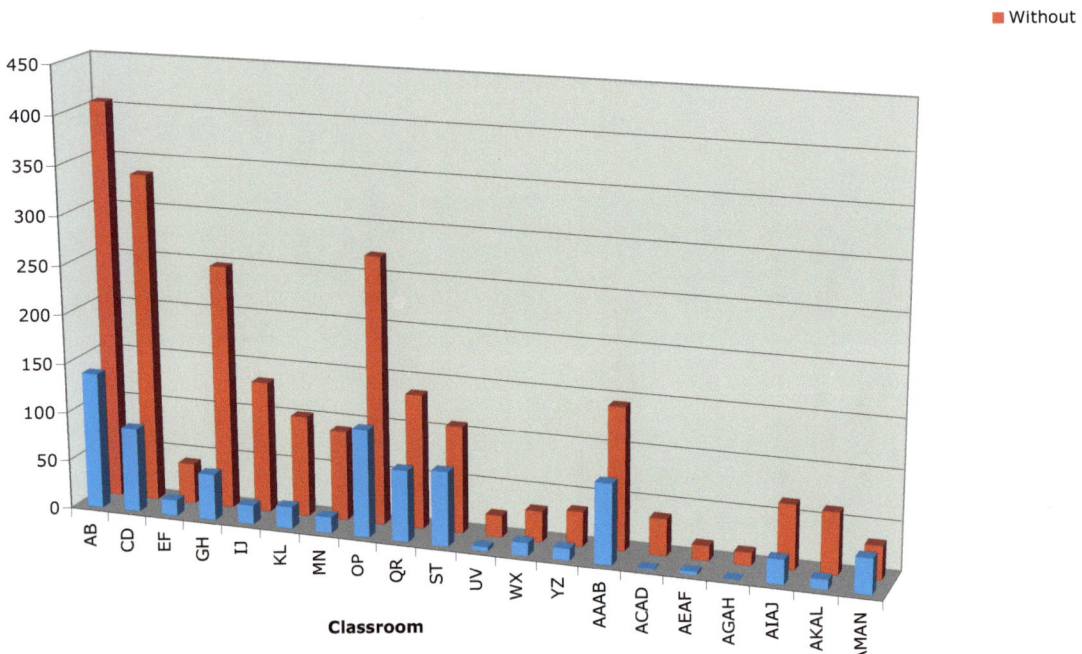

What does that look like with all those behaviors measured together? Glad you asked. I just so happen to have that chart to share. As you can see from the **blue**, (enough about the red) when midline exercises were conducted in the classrooms, all six behaviors being measured, decreased. The most interesting outcome was that most of those schools are still conducting midline exercises with their students.

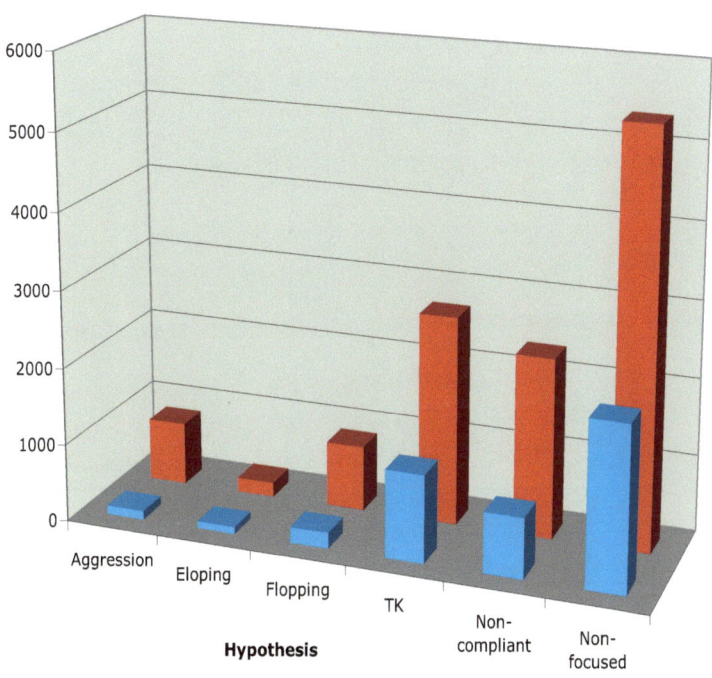

"The beginning is the most important part of the work."

Plato (427 – 347)

CHAPTER 2: NOW WHAT?

The next step is having a basic understanding on how our brain works. Let's begin with the left hemisphere (side). There are many great websites that can be used, a couple of my favorite are: '*Bain Made Simple*', which is located at http://brainmadesimple.com and '*KidsHealth*' which breaks information down nicely, located at https://kidshealth.org/en/kids/brain.html.

However, for my purposes two charts that briefly outlines the interactive right brain vs. left brain functions, and the regions and parts of the brain were created. My object is to keep everything very simple. Nonetheless, there are some really excellent articles, graphs, and charts that can be found by Googling 'brain'.

Characteristics of the right and left brain.

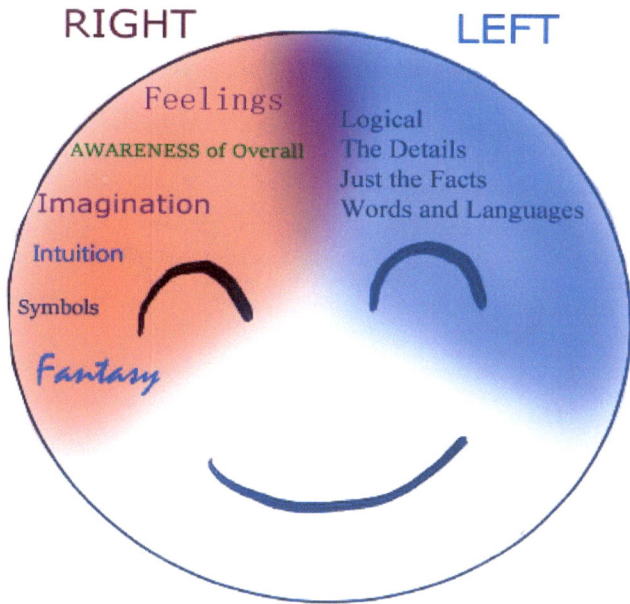

Regions and Parts of the Brain.

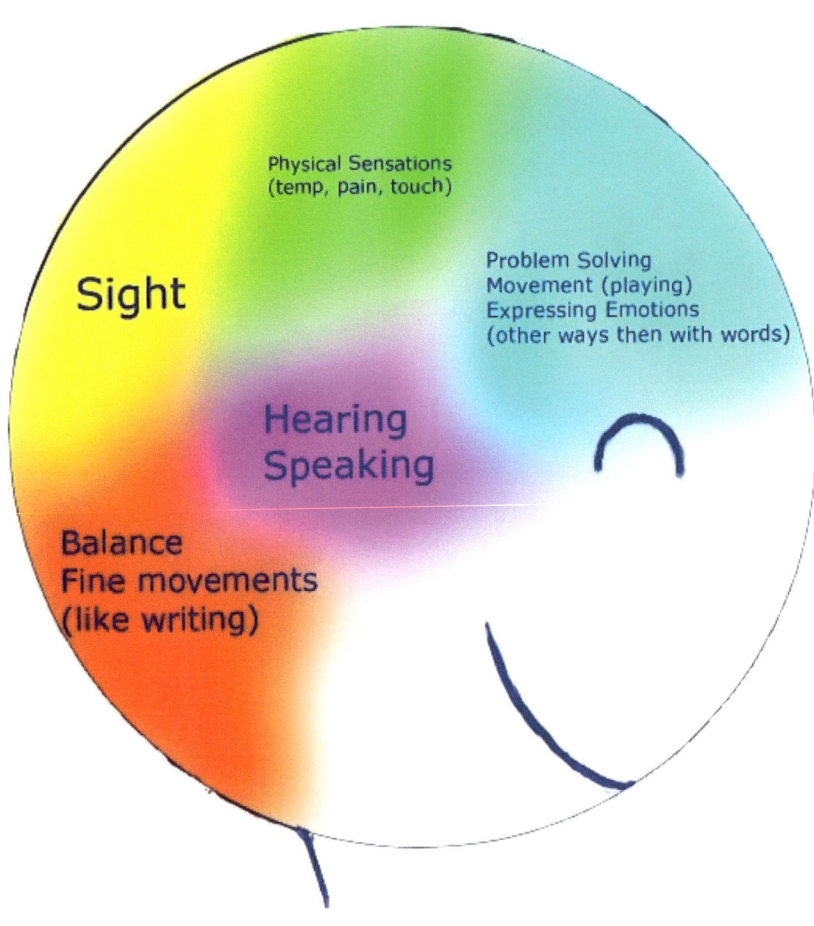

By the way, you are doing great taking in all this information. So, let us bring all this information together.

Now you can see that with all these moving parts and responsibilities with our brains (left, right, the regions, and parts) how can we support communication among these systems so that they can participate together?

Personally, I do not feel there is just one answer, but rather that getting the brain system in a calm place to send and receive information, gives a child the best opportunity for success.

At last, this brings me to why I have written this book, to introduce the set of five simple midline exercises that I have put together with an amazing team of women (Lori Eller, Kimberley Lee, and Chanel Dustow).

Those midline exercises (MLE) are listed in my last chapter, chapter three. They include the written and visual instructions for five very simple midline exercises that can be performed anytime and anyplace (provided it is humanly possible).

I would like to leave you with these thoughts:

Simple promotes understanding.
Understanding leads to awareness.
Awareness provides a calmness to our place within our systems.

"Perhaps they are not stars, but rather openings in heaven where the love of our lost ones pours through and shines down upon us to let us know they are happy."

- Eskimo Proverb

CHAPTER 3: THE H.A.P.P.Y. EXERCISES

Before we get started it, is important you check with a physician regarding your health. Also, at any time should something not feel right, stop and consult a physician. Please know that there are several other bilateral/ midline exercises available to you. These exercises that I have put together to create the concept of H.A.P.P.Y. are based off of my research. Also, for brain injured individuals, please make sure the team responsible for your well-being, support these exercises before beginning.

Please enjoy and be H.A.P.P.Y.

Hug me Time

1. Arms stretched out, standing tall, fingers extended.

    Hold for the count of 1... 2... 3.

2. Now, Hug Yourself – arms crossed in front, touching opposite hand to opposite shoulder, squeezing hug.

    Hold for the count of 1... 2... 3.

3. Release.
4. Repeat steps 1, 2 and 3 - three times.

    Note: Give each arm a chance to be on top when you hug.

    Smile, you did a great job!

Angel Taps

1. Standing tall, take a deep breath, filling your lungs. Imagine they're huge balloons filling up, then, release out slowly. Repeat three times.

2. <u>RIGHT SIDE:</u> Hands on hips, point your right big toe towards the ground in front of you. Tap your big toe on the ground gently. Slowly move that tapping toe to the left side of your body so it looks like you are tapping out a half moon shape in front of your body. Then tap your toe back towards your right side.

Smile, you're doing a great job!

3. <u>LEFT SIDE:</u> Repeat hands on hips, **BUT** point your left big toe towards the ground in front of you. Tap your big toe on the ground gently. Slowly move that tapping toe to the right side of your body so it looks like you are tapping out a half moon shape in front of your body. Then, tap your toe back towards your left side.

    Smile, you did a great job!

4. Repeat steps 2 and 3 - three times.

Positive Pose

1. Standing tall, take a deep breath in, filling your lungs to huge balloons, release out slowly. Repeat three times

2. <u>RIGHT SIDE:</u> Swing your right foot over in front of your body and tuck that foot in so that your baby toes are touching. Hold for the count of 1... 2... 3. Now, swing back so that your big toes are next to each other.

    Smile, you're doing a great job!

3. <u>LEFT SIDE:</u> Swing your left foot over in front of your body and tuck that foot in so that your baby toes are touching. Hold for the count of 1... 2... 3. Now, swing back so that your big toes are next to each other.

4. Repeat steps 1, 2 and 3 - three times.

    Smile, you did a great job!

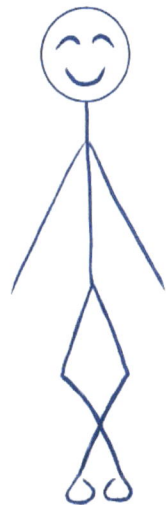

Perfect Job

1. Standing tall, fingers extended at your side.

2. <u>RIGHT SIDE:</u> Swing your right arm over to your left shoulder so that your right hand rests on your left shoulder. Turn, and look over at your right hand and say, "Good Job!"

    Then hold for the count of 1… 2… 3.

3. <u>LEFT SIDE:</u> Swing your left arm over to your right shoulder so that your left hand rests on your right shoulder. Turn, and look over at your left hand and say, "Good Job!"

    Hold for the count of 1… 2… 3.

4. Repeat steps 1, 2 and 3 - three times.

Smile, you did a great job!

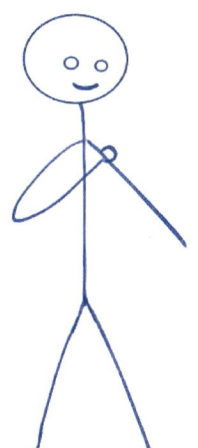 

You're a Star

1. Standing tall, take a deep breath in, filling your lungs to huge balloons. Release out, slowly. Repeat three times.

2. <u>RIGHT HAND:</u> Take your pointer finger and point in this order:
    i. to the sky above your left ear
    ii. to the ground in front of your right foot
    iii. to the sky above your right ear
    iv. to the ground in front of your left foot

    Smile, you're doing a great job!

3. <u>LEFT HAND</u> Take your pointer finger and point in this order:
    v. to the sky above your right ear
    vi. to the ground in front of your left foot
    vii. to the sky above your left ear
    viii. to the ground in front of your right foot

4. Repeat steps 2 and 3 - three times.

    Smile, you did a great job!

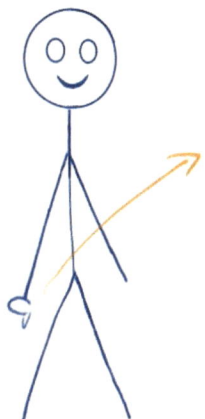

REFERENCES/ RESOURCES

American Kinesiology Association (AKA)   omicsonline.org

American Kinesiotherapy Association   akta.org

Brain Gym   braingym.org

Dustow, J., (2009), Autism Project of Dr. Jennifer Dustow. Lambert Academic Publishing, ISBN-NR 978-3-8383-1616-1 Number 1697 Translated into 31 languages.

Dustow, J., (2006), Bilateral exercises decrease "off task" behavior in special needs preschoolers on the Island of Oahu, Hawaii; *Brain Gym Journal*. 21(1), 4, 10-11.

Dustow, J., (2007), Bilateral Exercises that Cross the Midline Decrease Off Task Behavior in Preschool Children Diagnosed Under the Autism Spectrum On the Island of Oahu. ProQuest 2008, ISBN 978-0-549-58992

Davis, H., (2016), What Does an Occupational Therapist Actual do?, June 1, 2016, article published with The Guardian Newspaper under the Lifestyle section of the newspaper.

Jones, Scott, (2002), Brain Made Simple, http://brainmadesimple.com

Nemours Foundation (1995), KidsHealth, Reviewed by Dr. Steven Dowshen
https://kidshealth.org/en/kids/brain.html

ABOUT THE AUTHOR

Dr. Jennifer Dustow holds a doctorate in Educational Leadership and is a Cognitive Behavioral Learning Specialist. Through her private practice, she has helped families, organizations, and companies with her compassionate problem-solving approach. She is also known for her international cutting edge research in autism (currently printed in 27 languages). M.L.E. is the outcome from that research, along with several years of creating behavioral programs that have redirected and reduced misunderstood behaviors.

Dr. Jennifer Dustow serves as President of Cornerstone Educational Preschool, the non-profit preschool for children diagnosed under the autism spectrum, founded by her in 2007.

On the island of Lanai in Hawaii, she conducts trainings for parents, service providers, educational personnel, trainers, and the general public who wish to know more.

A YouTube video short can be found at:
https://youtu.be/rm5l6RhMuUY

www.ingramcontent.com/pod-product-compliance
Lightning Source LLC
Chambersburg PA
CBHW042125040426
42450CB00002B/69